ILLUSTRATED BIOGRAPHY FOR KIDS

ISAAC NEWTON

EXTRAORDINARY SCIENTIST

WHO CHANGED THE WORLD

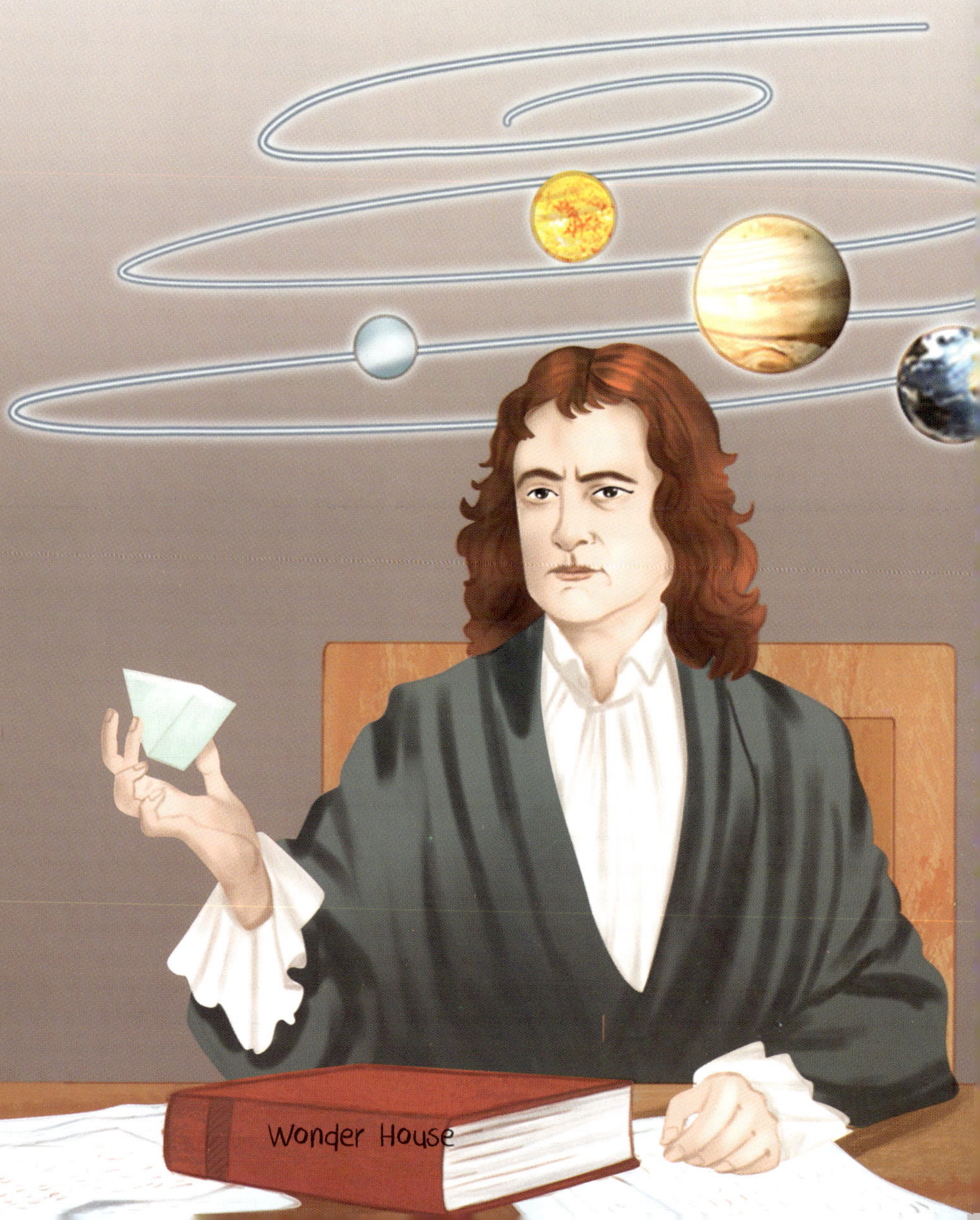
Wonder House

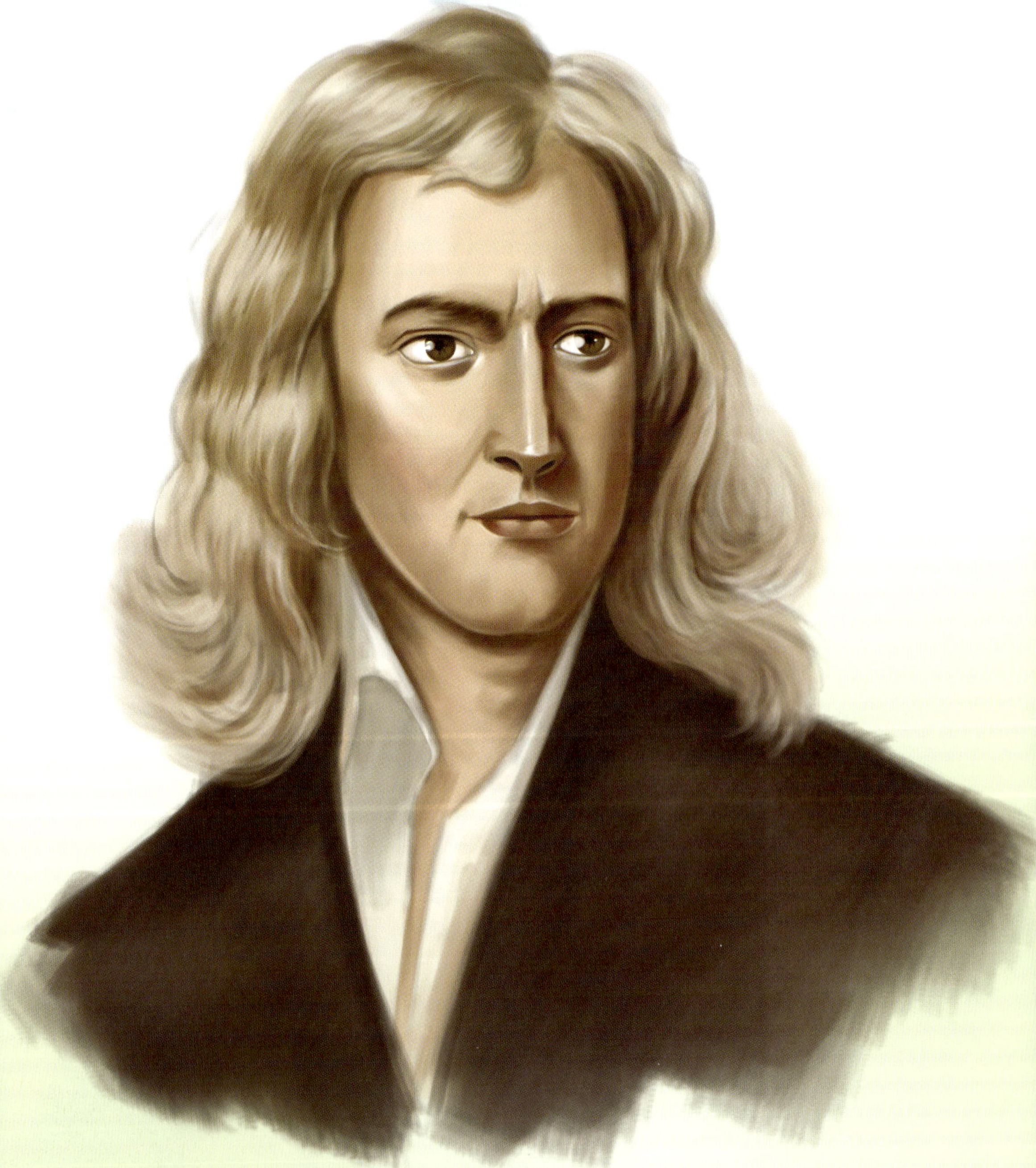

NEWTON, THE INCREDIBLE GENIUS

Isaac Newton (1643–1727) was an English physicist, mathematician, astronomer, and theologian. He is credited as one of the greatest minds of the 17th century and an important figure in the philosophical revolution, also known as Enlightenment. He published his famous work, *Philosophiae Naturalis Principia Mathematica* (Mathematical Principles of Natural Philosophy) in 1687, which formed the basis of classical mechanics. He was a man of high intellect which is evident in his incredible discoveries of gravity, motion, optics, mathematics, and many more.

EARLY LIFE

Isaac Newton was born on 4 January 1643, in Woolsthorpe, a small village near Grantham, England. He was born a year after Galileo Galilei, another genius of the century, died. His father, also named Isaac, was an illiterate farmer who died three months before he was born.

Newton had a very lonely and difficult childhood, which resulted in psychotic tendencies in the later years of his life. After his father's death, his mother Hannah Ayscough Newton remarried and left 3 years old Isaac in the care of his maternal grandmother. This event had a significant impact on his psyche, which later manifested in deep insecurities and anxiety with regard to his work. Ironically, his stepfather also died within nine years of marriage, which led to the return of his mother to Woolsthorpe in 1653, but this time she didn't come alone. She brought her three children from the second marriage along with her.

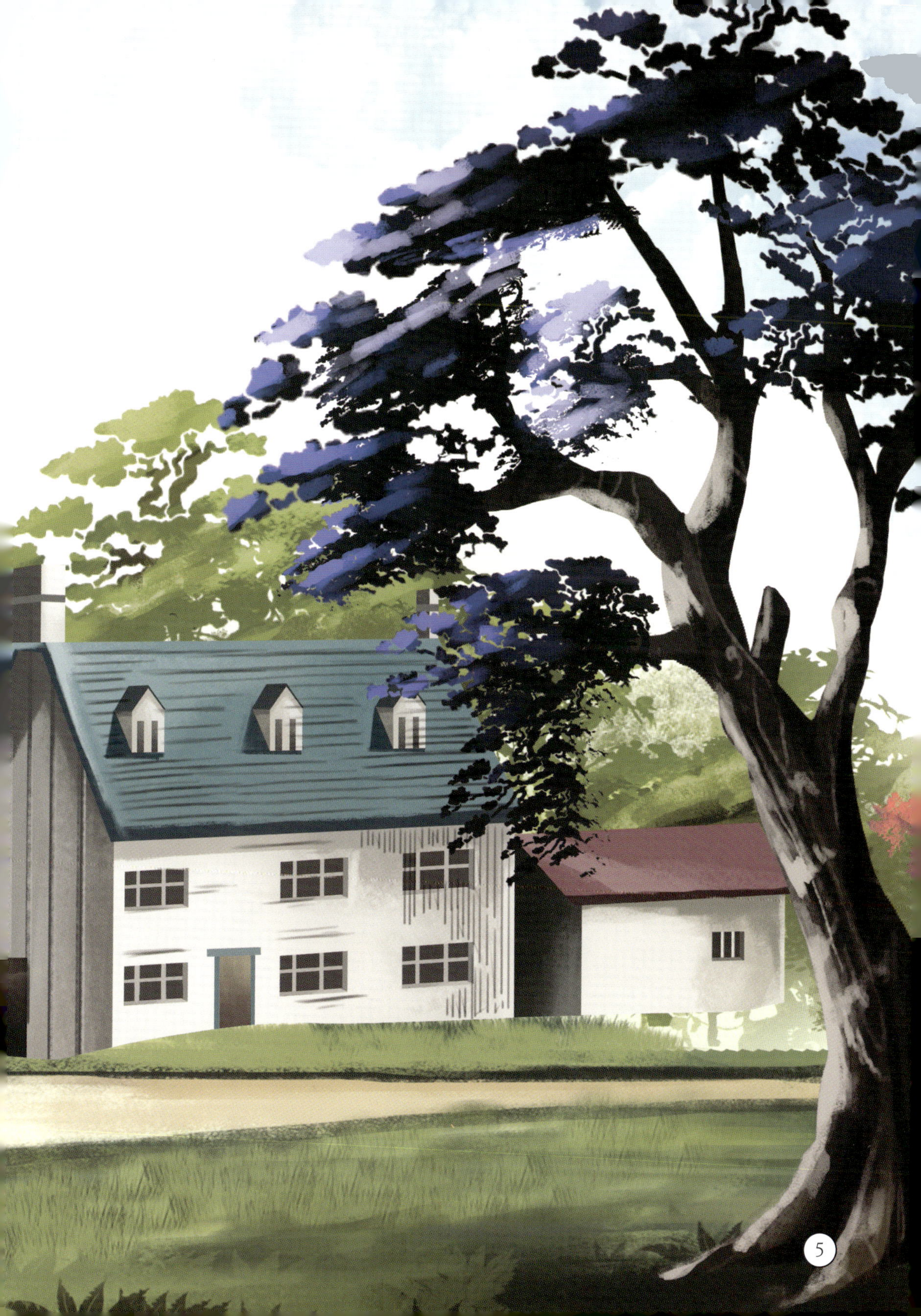

THE PLOY OF FATE

At the age of 12, Newton joined The King's School at Grantham, where he learned Greek and Latin along with some basic mathematics. However, he didn't showcase much interest in academics and received many complaints from his teachers.

His mother was a lady of reasonable wealth and property. Hence, she called Isaac back to Woolsthorpe to manage her estate, as elder

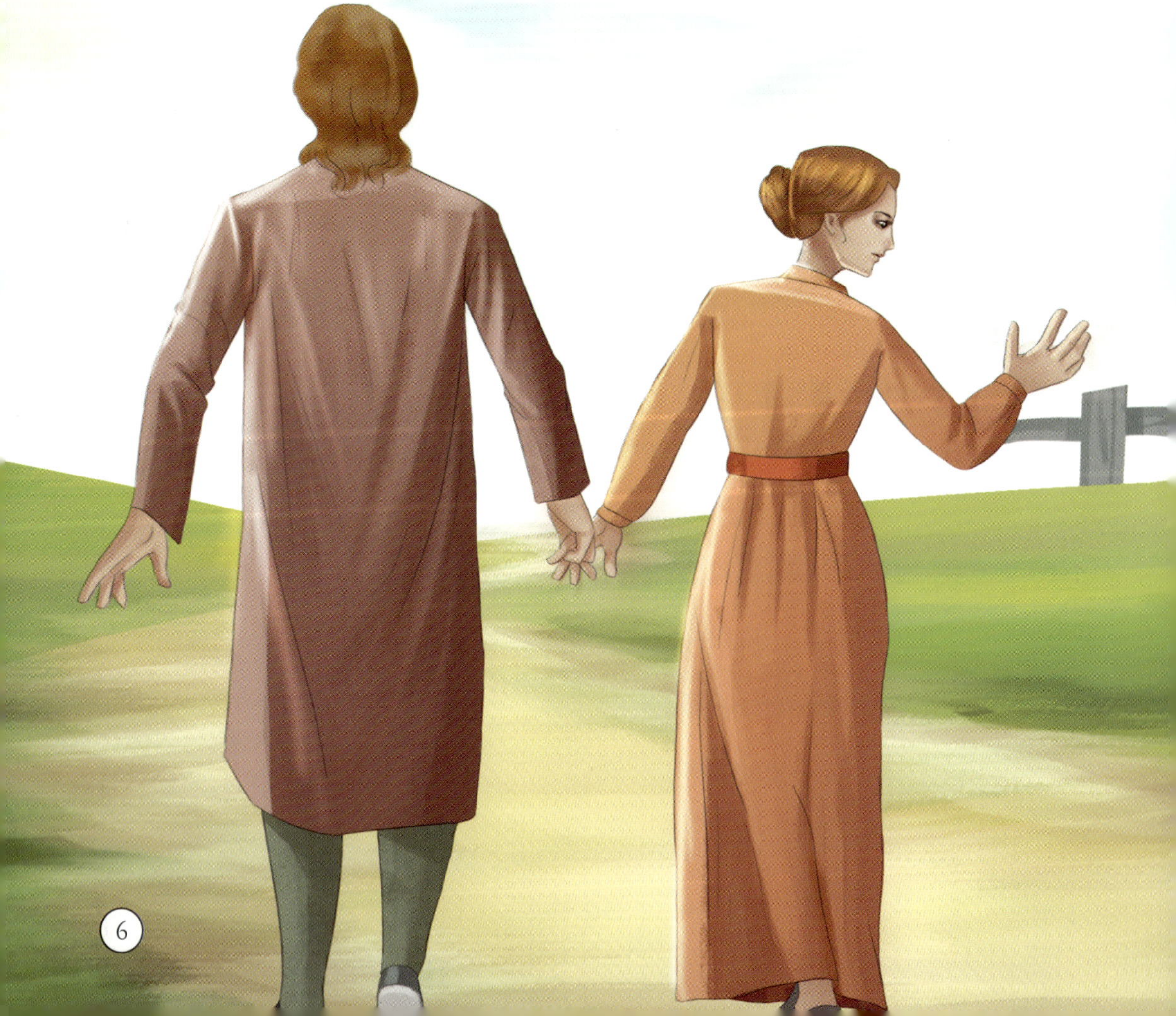

sons were supposed to do. But, fate had other plans. Newton found farming boring and showed no interest in running the family farm. It was only after persuasion from his headmaster at King's School, that his mother allowed him to return to his studies.

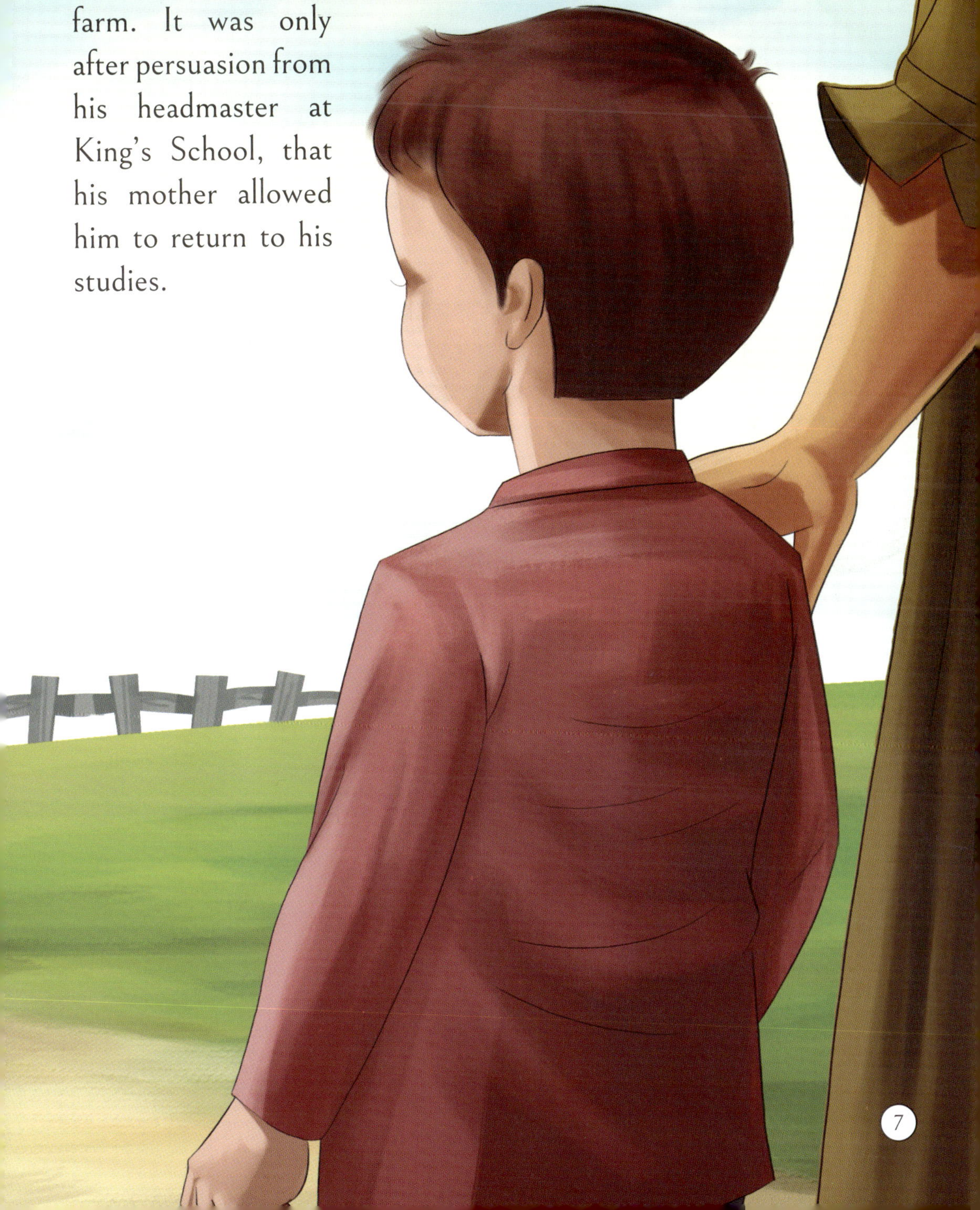

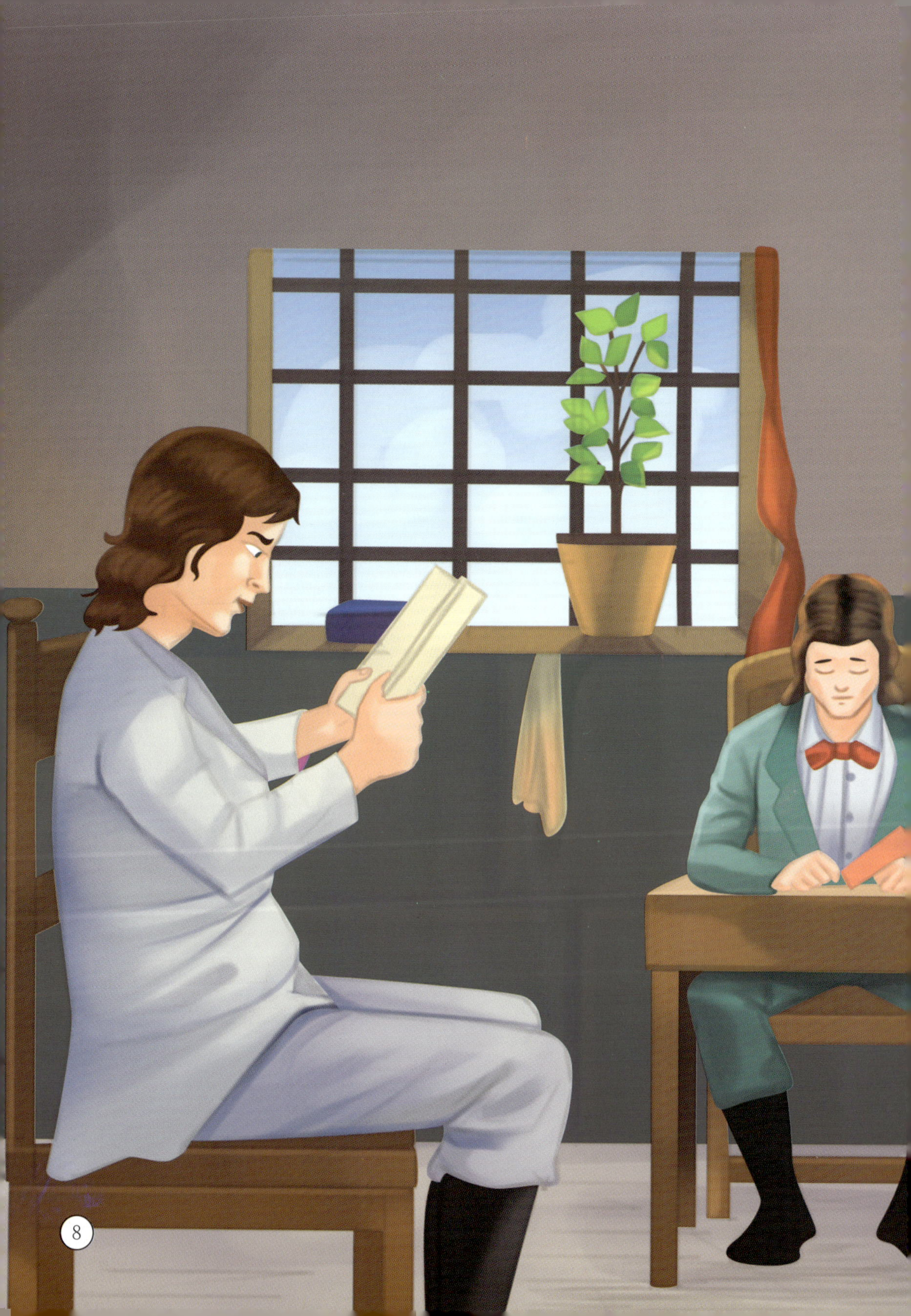

JOURNEY TO CAMBRIDGE

Newton entered Trinity College, Cambridge, on the recommendation of his uncle, who had himself studied there. When Isaac entered college, he was older than most of his classmates.

He entered college as a subsizar—a student who earned his allowances by attending to his fellow students, and doing their basic chores. He remained a subsizar till he attained a scholarship in 1664, which gave him four more years to stay at Cambridge till he finished his master's degree.

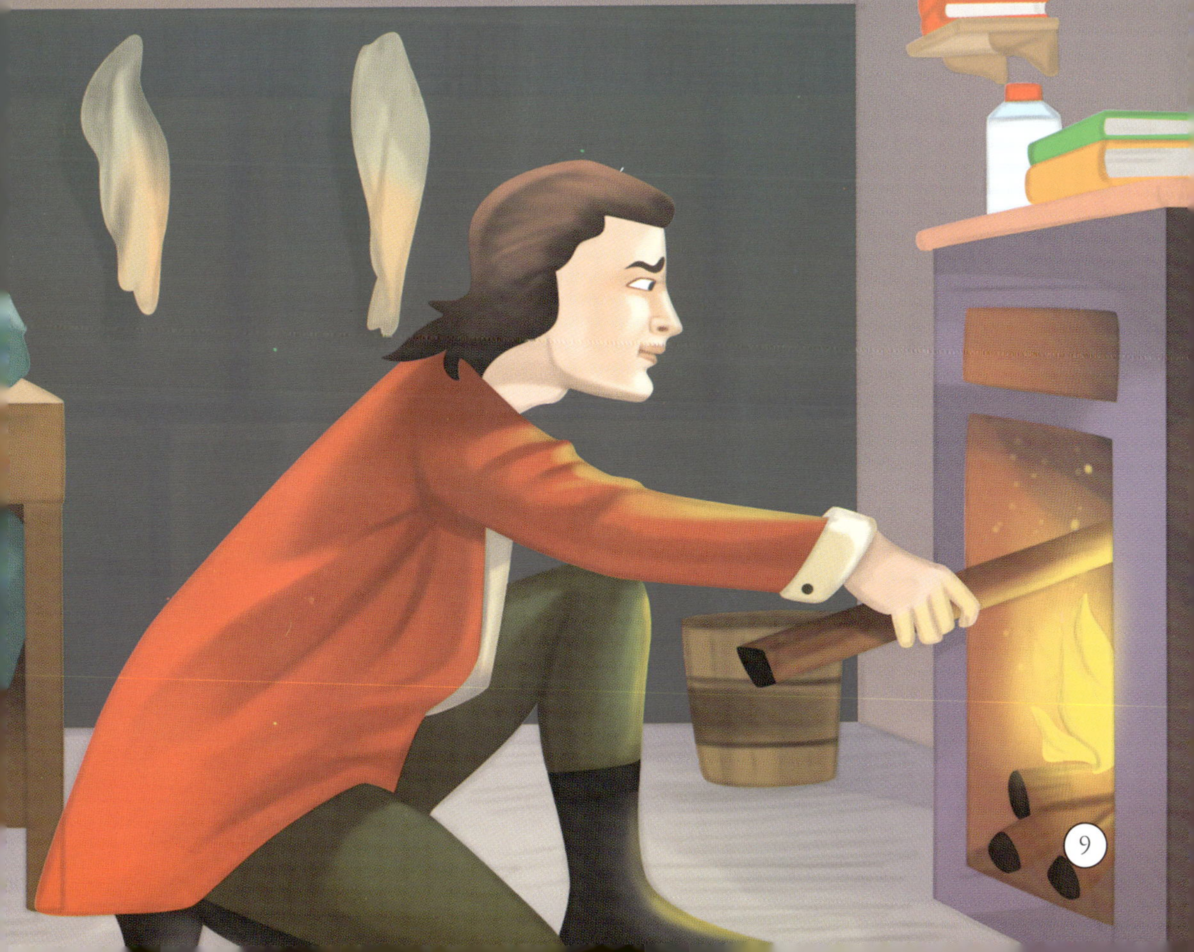

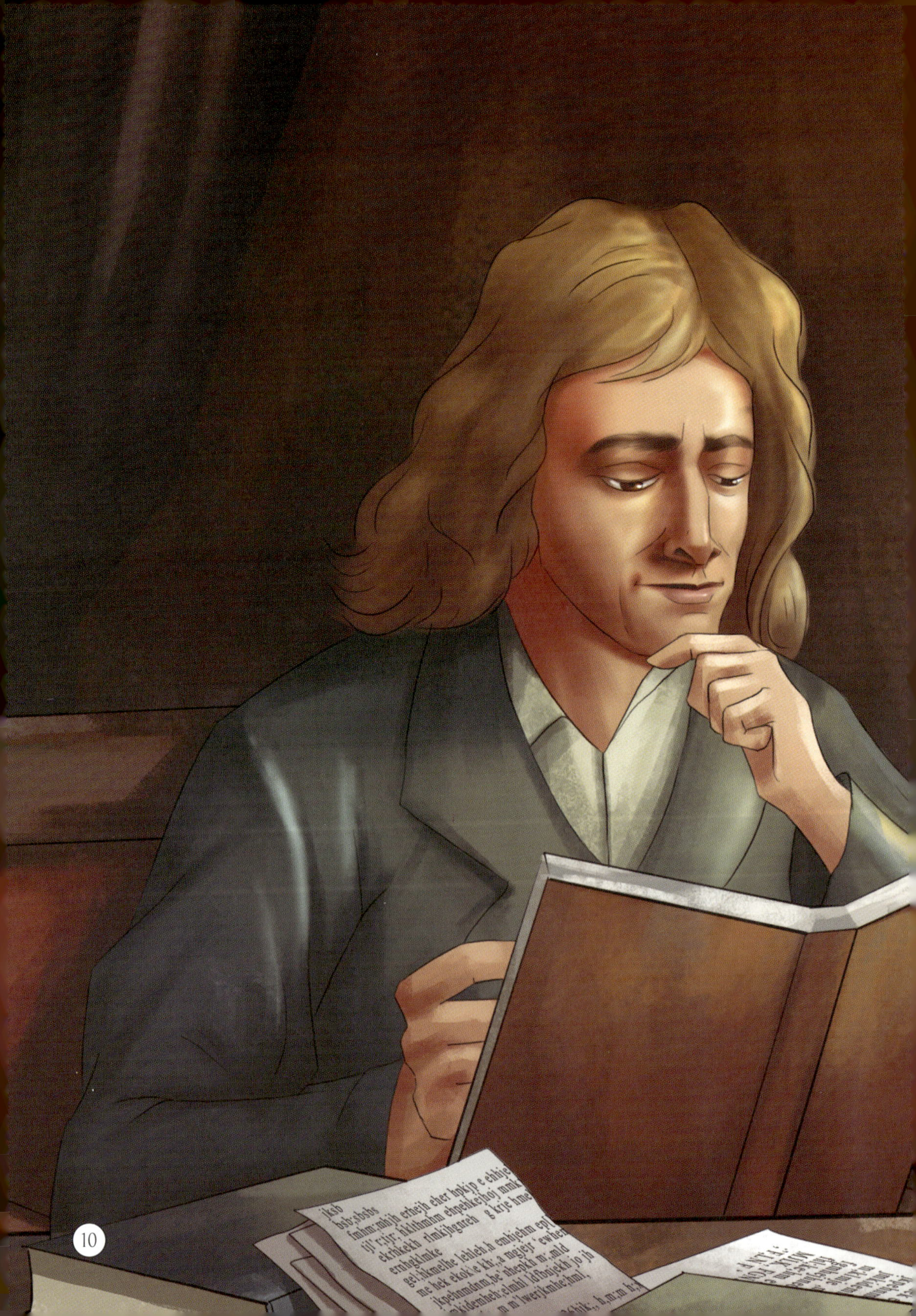

When Newton entered Cambridge, Scientific Revolution was already in motion and was advancing at a fast pace. The discoveries of Copernicus and Johannes Kepler had already laid the foundation for the heliocentric view of the world, which stated that the sun is the center of the universe, not earth as was popularly believed. The discoveries of Galileo and Descartes had already laid the foundation of the learnings based on scientific reason and logical principles.

These advances in the scientific realm had a profound impact upon Newton, he delved into these studies outside his rhetoric curriculum. He began reading beyond his standard module and enhanced his knowledge by reading the works of the greatest philosophers and mathematicians of the time. In 1665, Newton compiled his own theories in the form of notes and titled them *Quaestiones Quaedam Philosophicae* (Certain Philosophical Questions). The 'Quaestiones' proposes his conception of nature, which paved the way for the next revolution in the field of science.

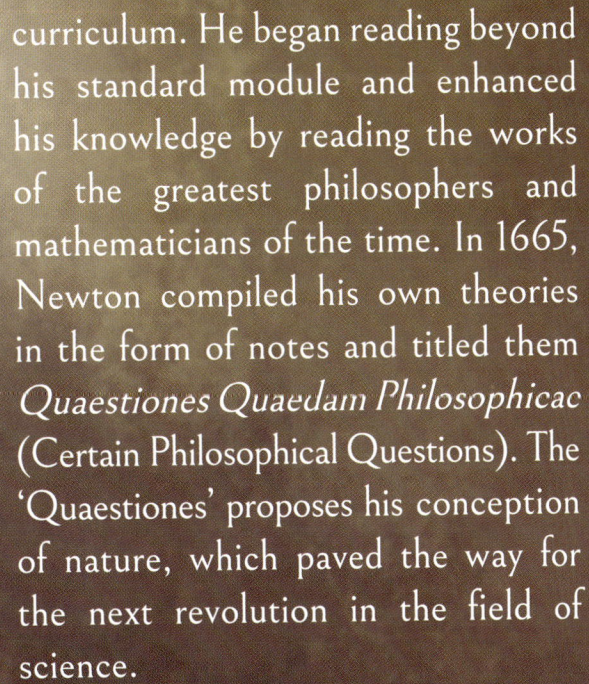

UNRAVELLING THE OCEANS OF TRUTH

Newton's progress as a scientific genius emerged during the time of the bubonic plague, when the universities were closed in the summer of 1665 for two years, and he was forced to go back to

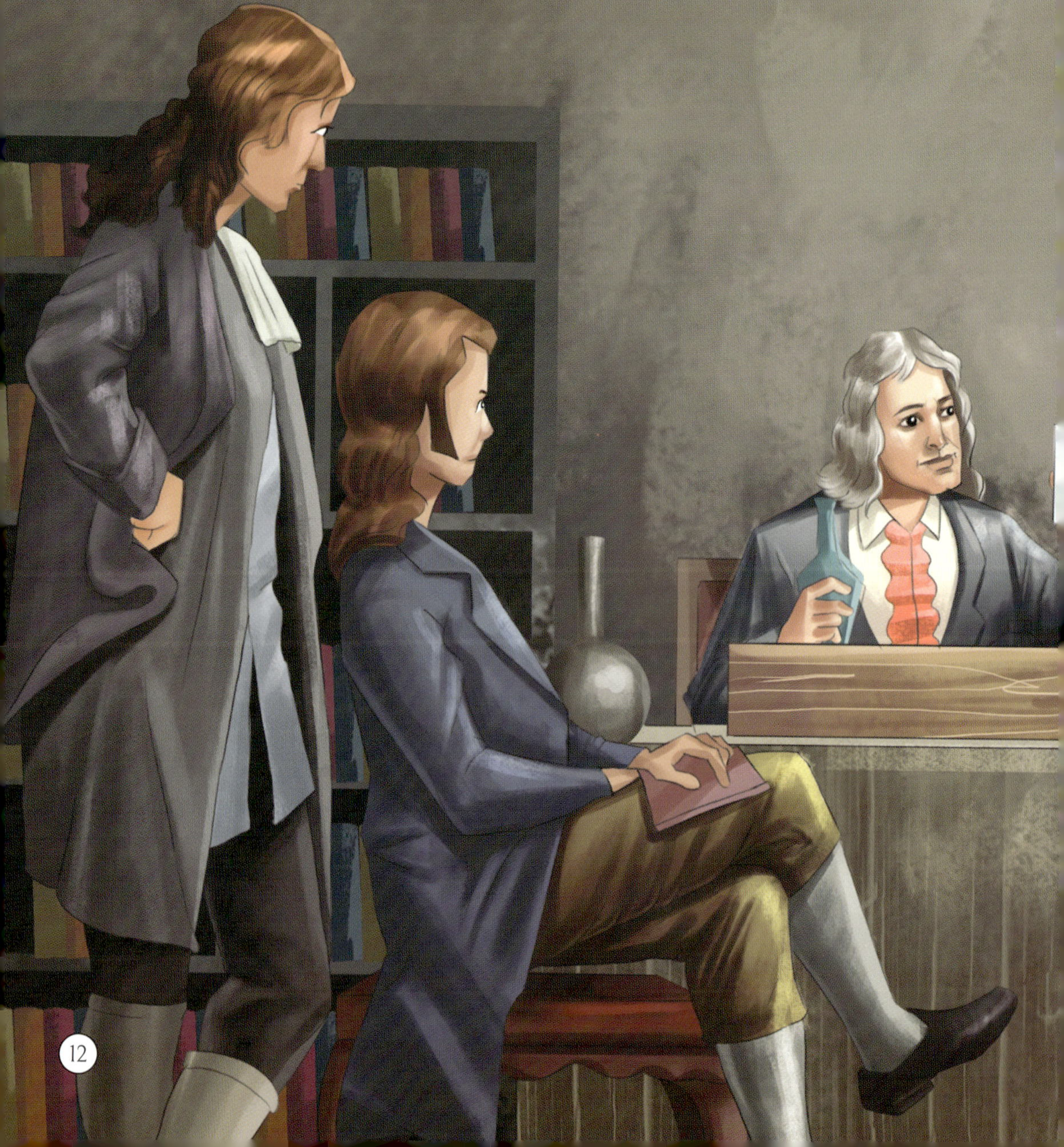

Woolsthorpe, Lincolnshire. In this period, he started his extensive study of astronomy, mathematics, optics, and physics. It was during this time that he laid the foundations of calculus, worked on his theory of colors and discovered the law of gravity.

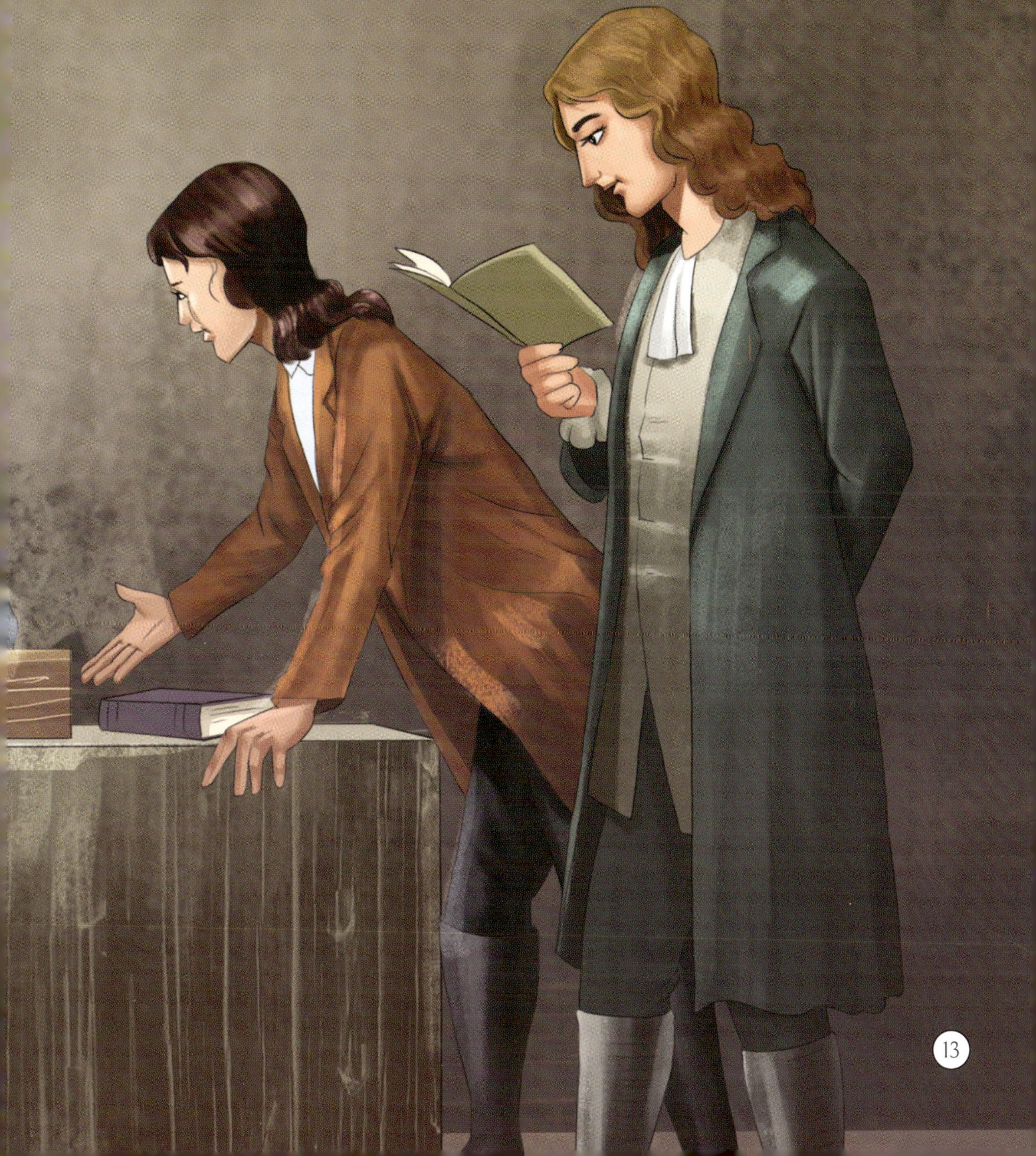

In 1667, the universities reopened, Newton returned to Cambridge and was elected as minor fellow at Trinity College. In 1669, he finished his master's degree. It was during this time that he wrote his famous treatise, *Ön Analysis by Infinite* series, one of the celebrated works of mathematics. In his treatise, Newton propounded his own wide-ranging results.

This was the first time that his work was acknowledged by the mathematics community. Later, he went on to become the Lucasian Professor of Mathematics at Cambridge.

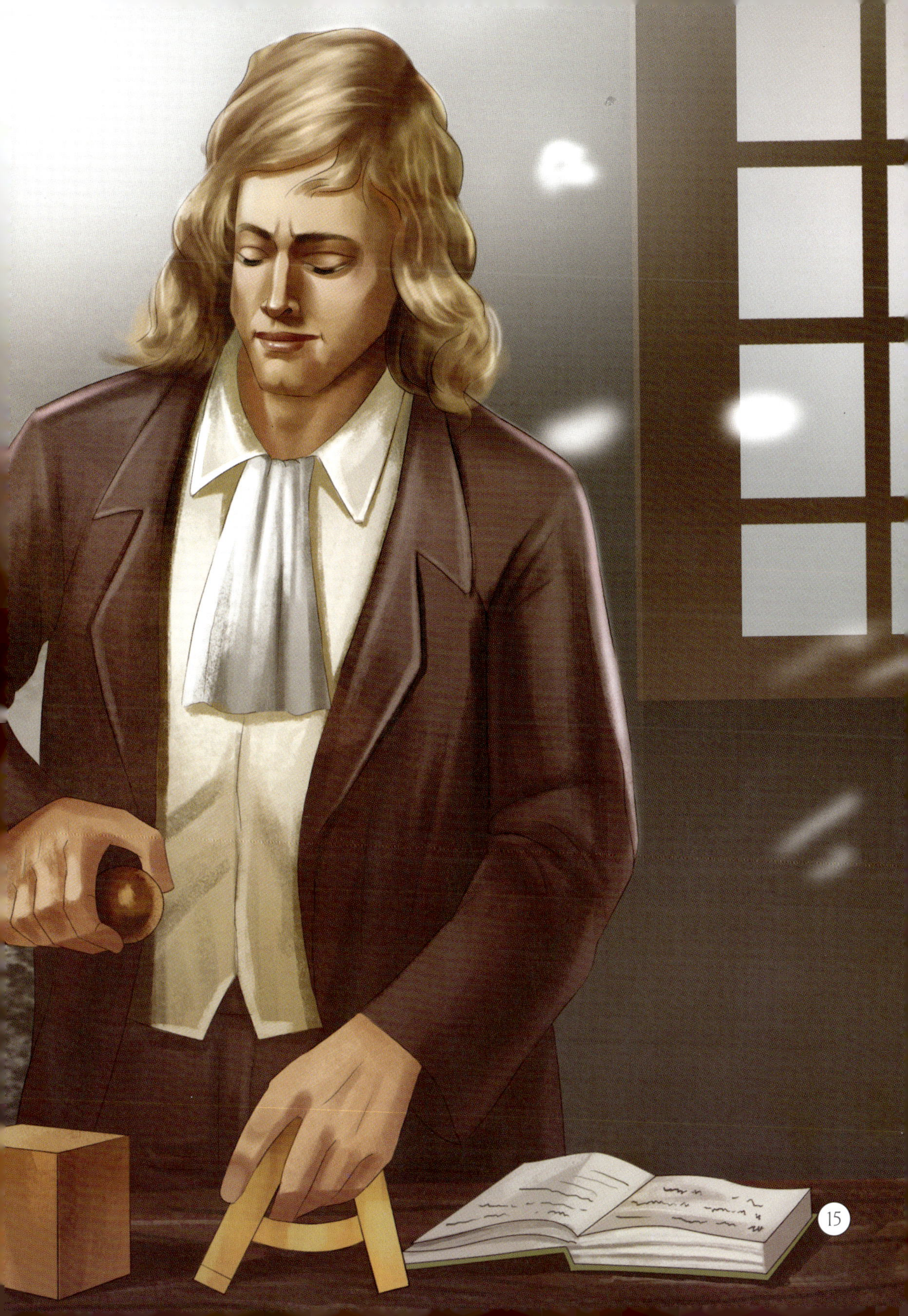

THE BATTLE OF CALCULUS

Newton is credited with many mathematical discoveries such as the generalized binomial theorem, Newton identities, methods, and the classification of cubic plane curves, to name a few. Despite, his extraordinary intellect, Newton abstained from publishing his work for the fear of criticism. His highly obsessive attitude towards his work landed him in many disputes, which further compounded his self-isolation at a later stage in life.

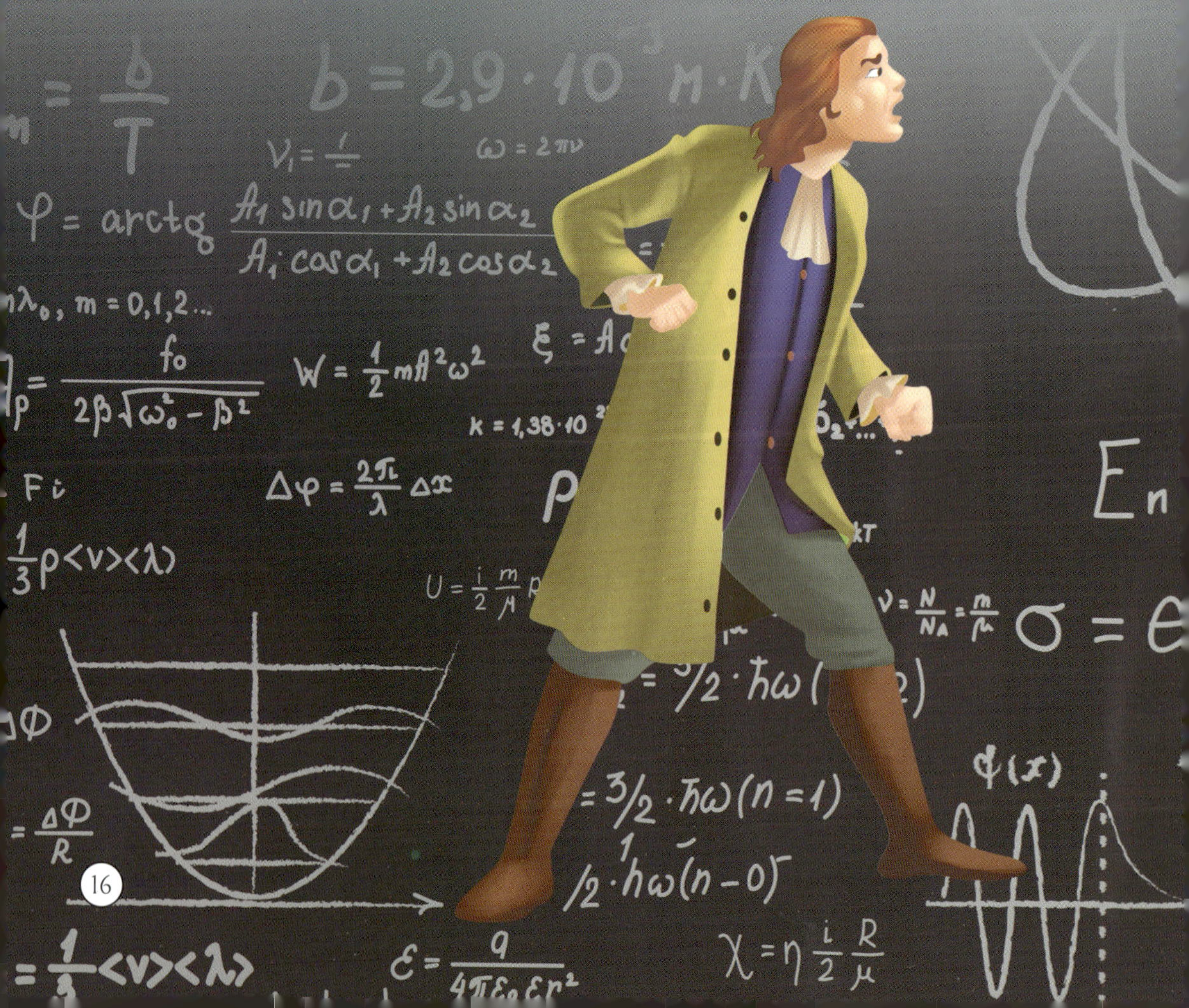

One of the most controversial ones was his conflict with Gottfried Leibniz, a German philosopher, over who invented calculus. Though Leibniz was the first to publish his work, but Newton's supporters accused him of plagiarism. This conflict had a great impact on their relationship, which had deteriorated beyond measure, and continued till Leibniz's death in 1716. Although today, modern historians believe that both Leibniz and Newton developed calculus independently using different mathematical notations.

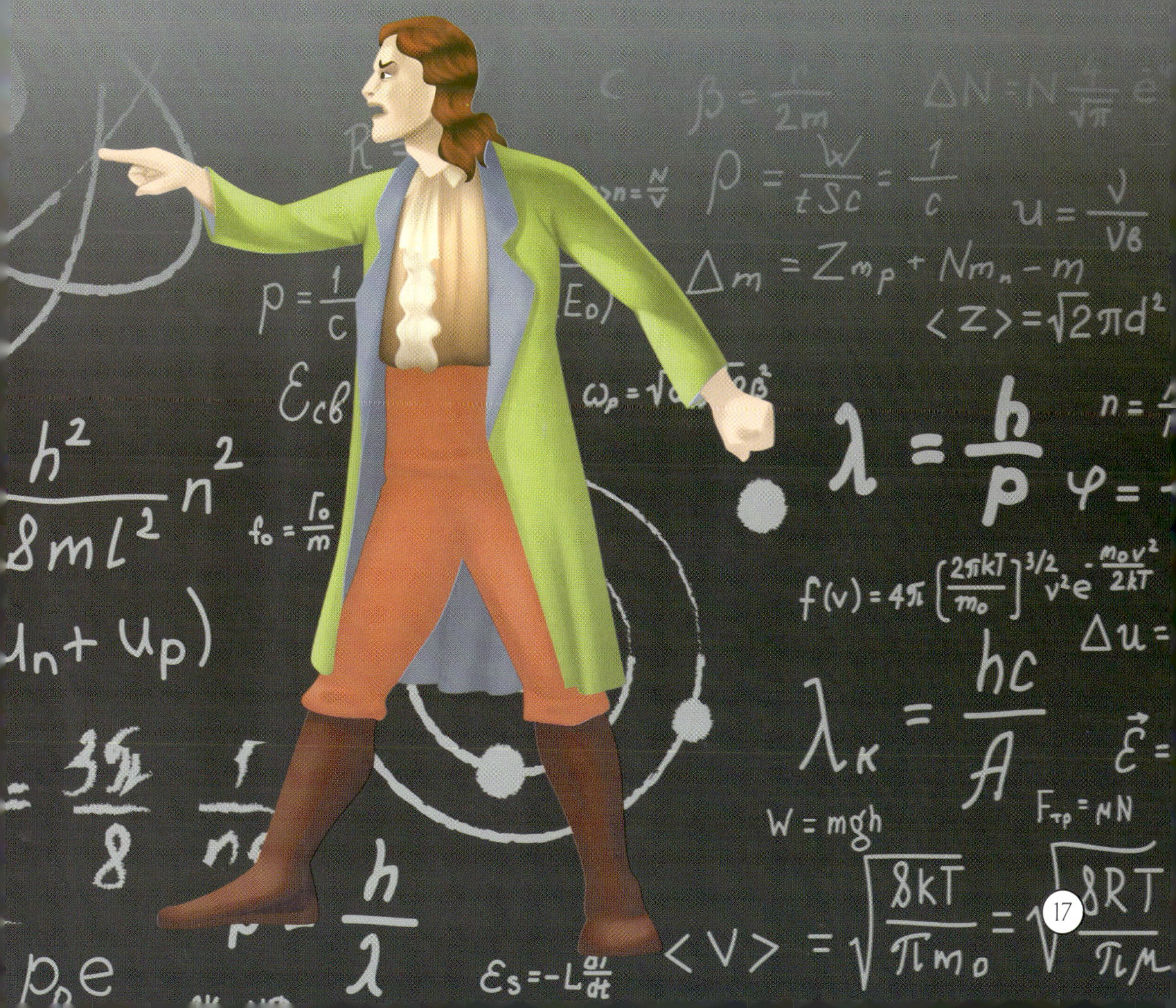

W = mgh
F_тр = μN
λ = h/p
λ_к = hc/A
Δm = Zm_p + Nm_n − m
<Z>=√2πd²

STANDING ON THE SHOULDERS OF GIANTS

Newton's Lucasian chairmanship exempted him from necessary tutoring and gave him room to indulge in more private research in alchemy, chemistry and

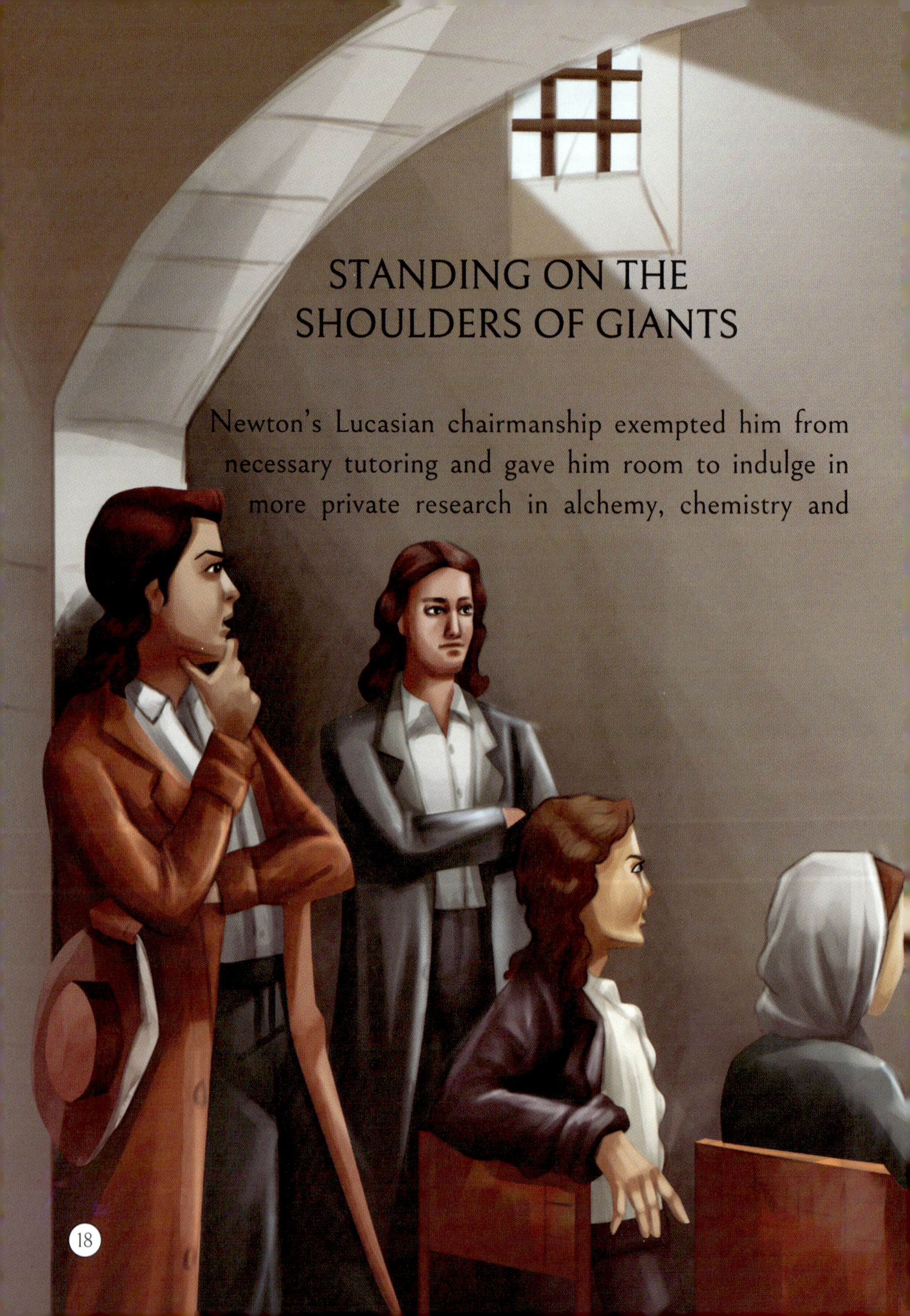

theology. He purchased scientific instruments for his research and devoted much of his time to private studies.
As a chairman, his duty was to deliver annual lectures. He chose his research in optics as the first topic of his discourse. His lectures developed into 'The Essay of Colors' which were later compiled into his first book of *Opticks*.

Newton is also known for the development of 'The Theory of Colors'. He investigated the concept of refraction of light and scientifically demonstrated that white light was composed of seven visible colors; the beautiful colors which we see in a rainbow.

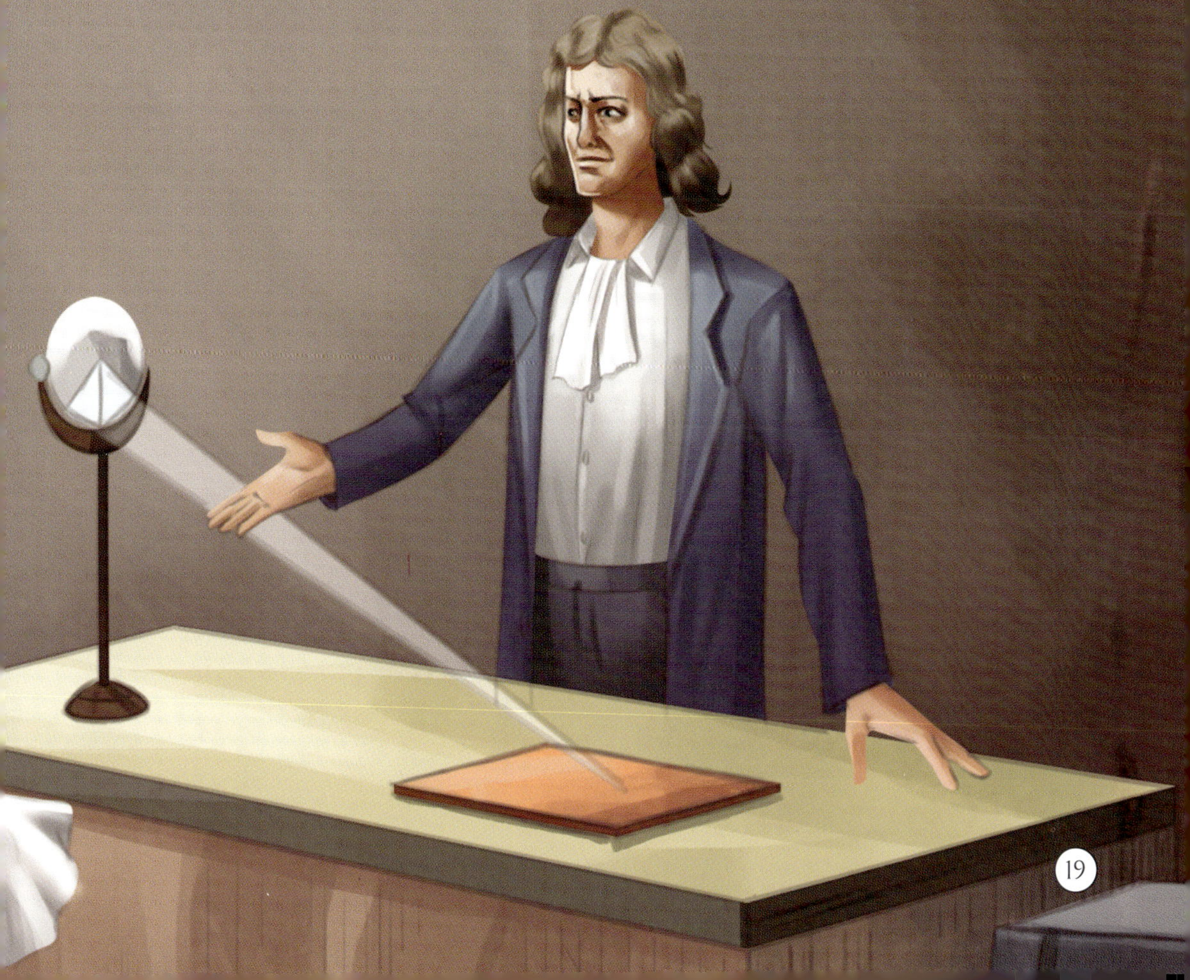

In 1668, Newton achieved another scientific feat by constructing the first reflecting telescope. The telescope was about eight-inches long and gave clear and large images for study. He extensively used this telescope for his research studies in optics, and to prove his findings of the theory of light and color.

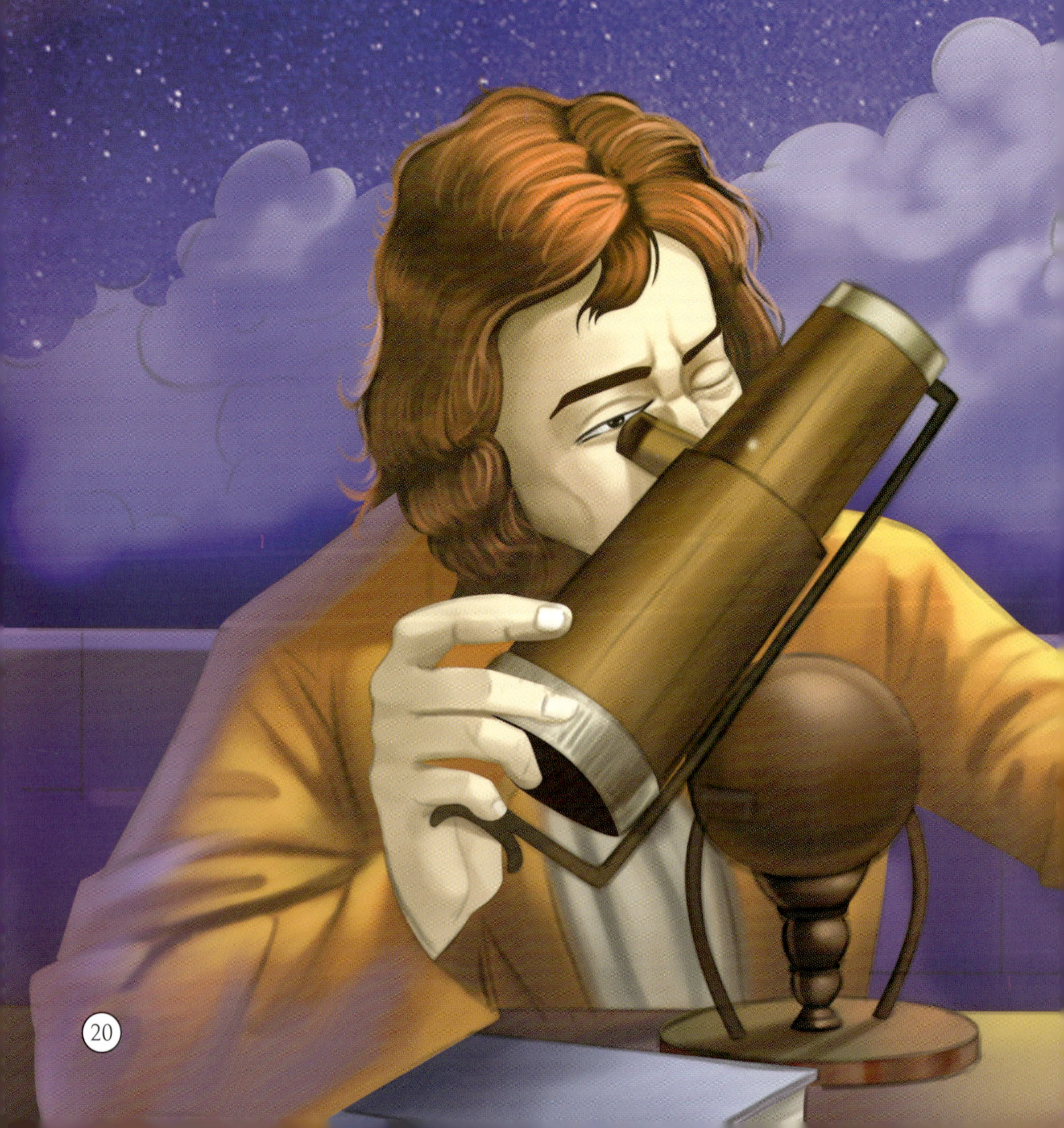

In 1671, he demonstrated his reflecting telescope in front of the Royal Society, that gave him a major boost and a much needed encouragement to publish his notes on light, optics and color for the general public.

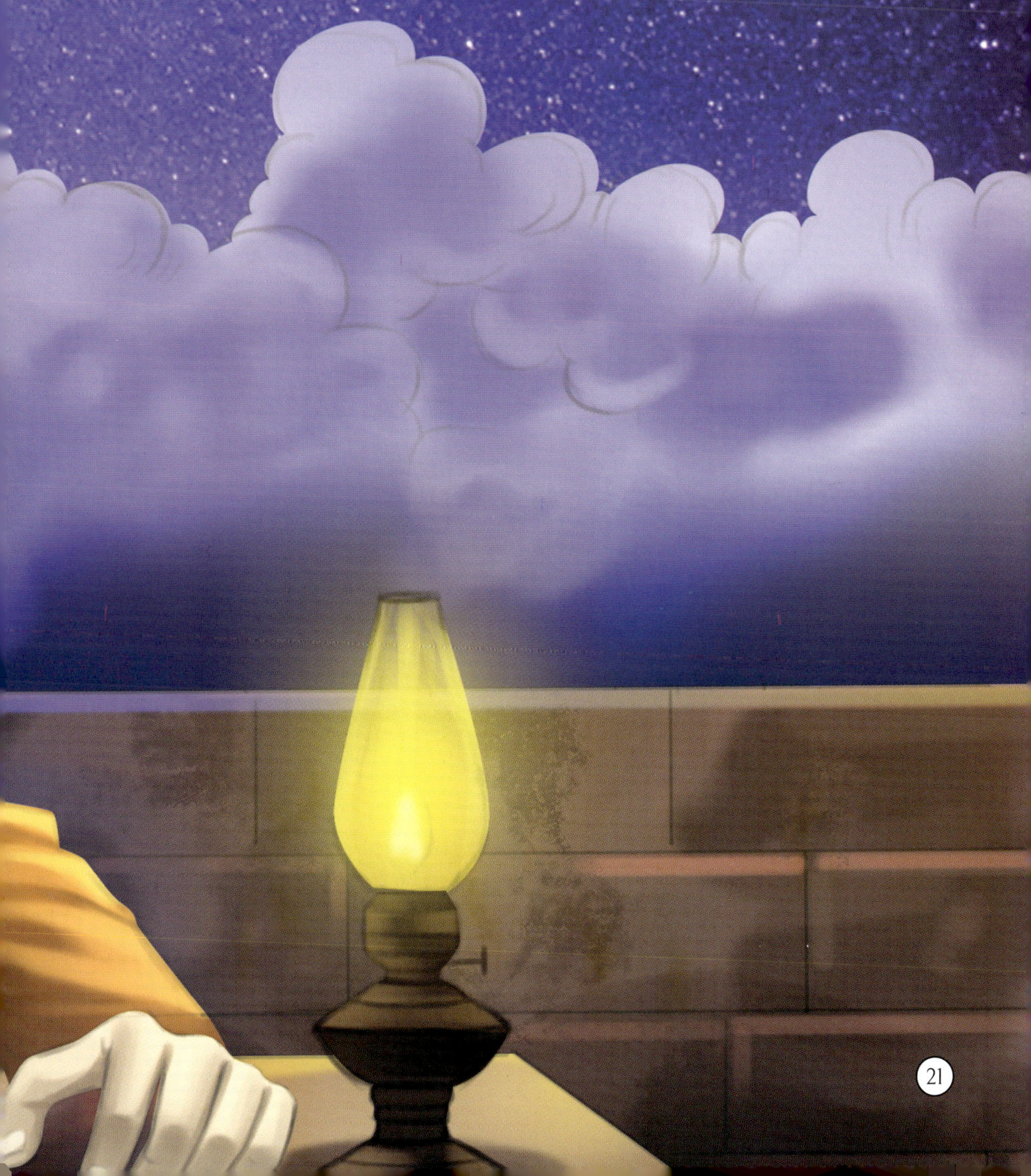

CULMINATION OF THE SCIENTIFIC REVOLUTION

Newton published *Principia or Mathematical Principles of Natural Philosophy* in 1687 with some encouragement from English astronomer Edmund Halley. The book has been acclaimed as the most influential work in physics.

It is credited to have laid the foundation for classical mechanics. In his work, Newton established the three laws of motion and the universal law of gravity. These laws prepared the groundwork for describing the relation between objects, the forces acting upon them and the resulting motion.

Principia led Newton to the heights of stardom in the scientific community and earned him international acclaim for his findings. His discoveries are regarded as the most important work in modern science as they contributed to many advances, especially during the Industrial Revolution.

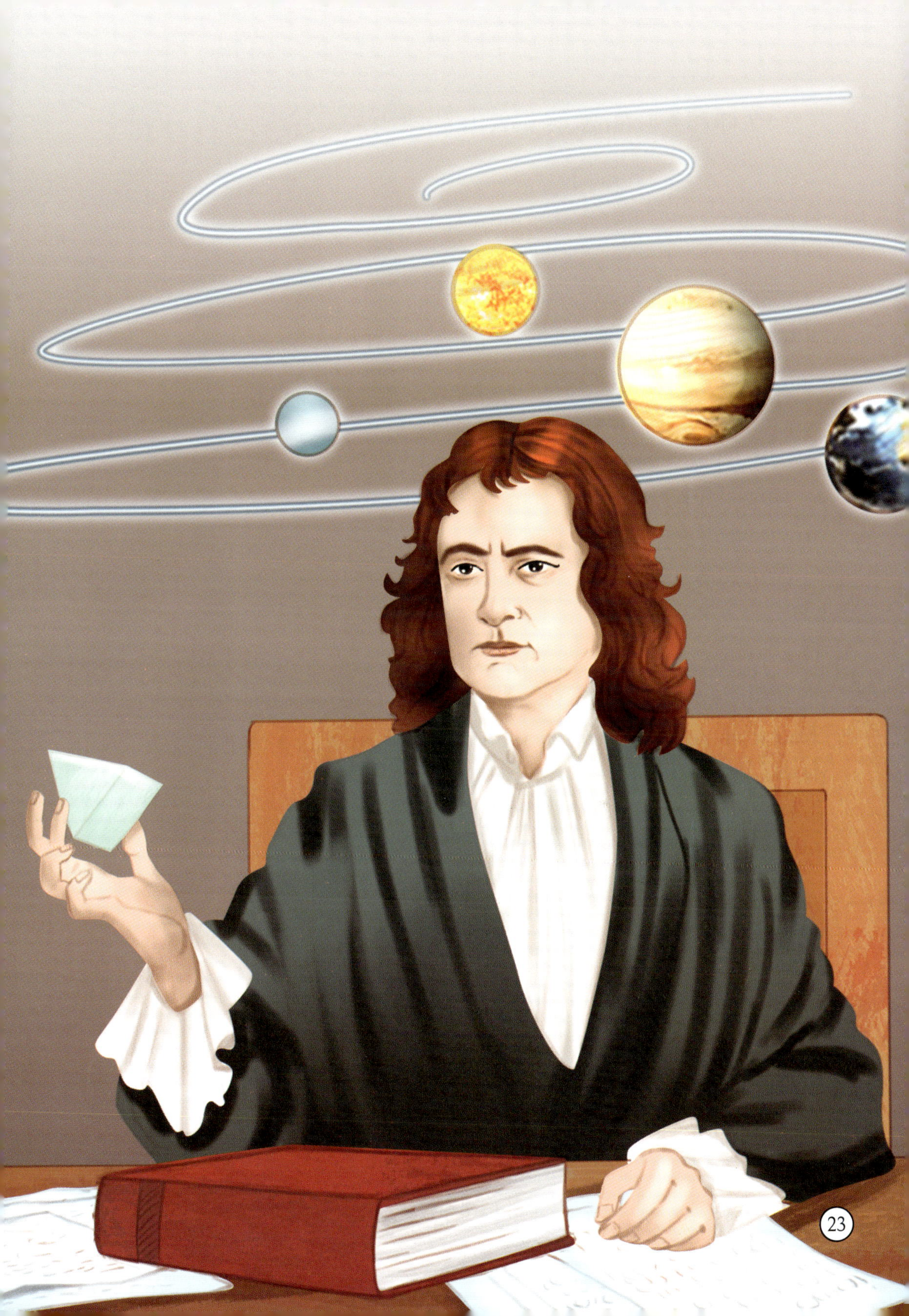

WHAT GOES UP MUST COME DOWN

It is widely and popularly believed that Newton found inspiration for his most famous discovery—Newton's law of universal gravitation, while sitting under an apple tree. The incident took place between 1665 and 1667, when the colleges were closed in the backdrop of the Great Plague.

As the legend goes, Newton was sitting under an apple tree when an apple hit his head, it made him wonder; why the apple fell downward and not in any other direction. Hence, it inspired him to come up with the law of gravity.

The law of gravity helped in explaining almost every other motion plying in the universe such as the revolution of planets around the sun, how the moon revolves around the earth or how the comets revolve in their elliptical orbits around the sun.

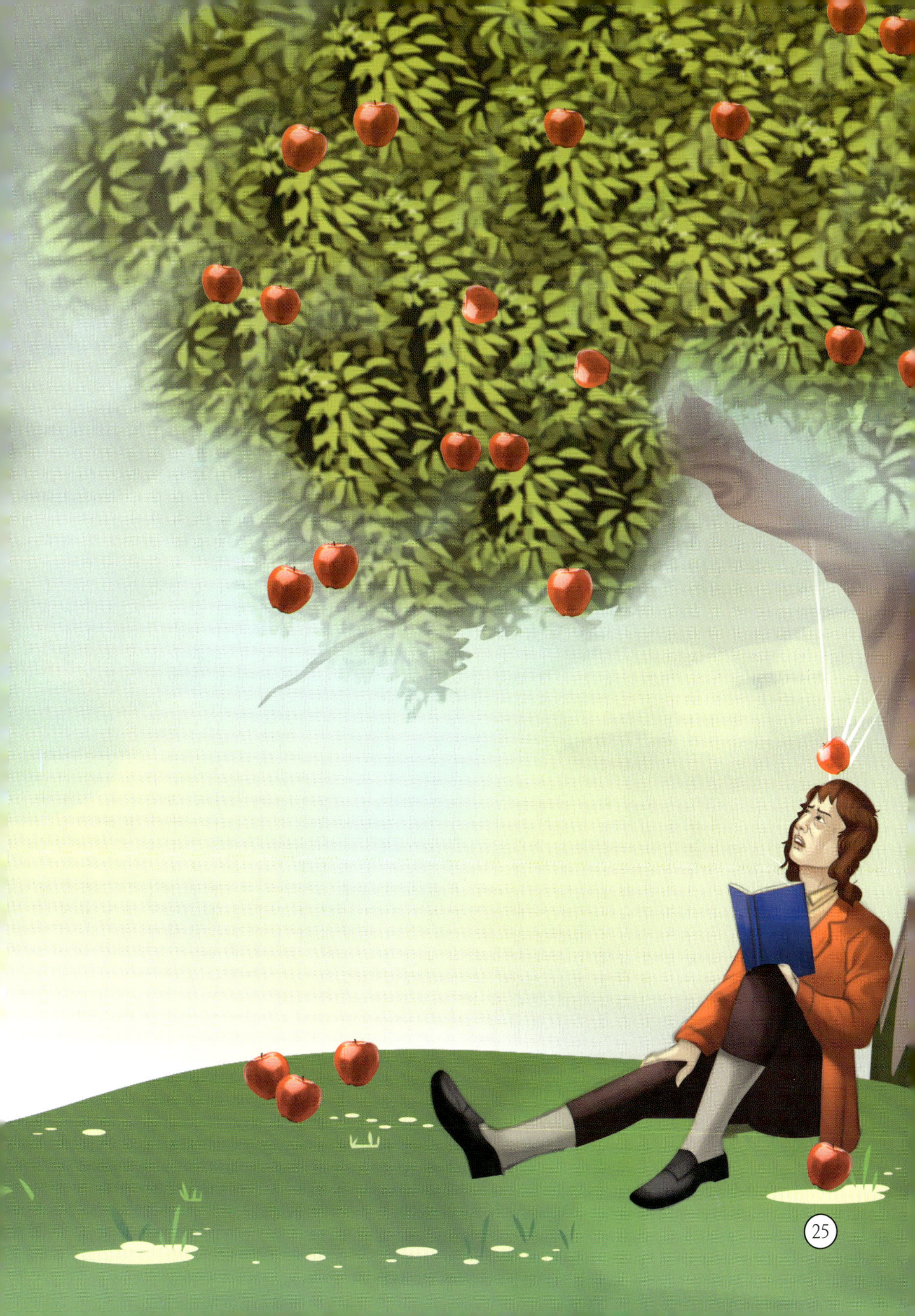

EXPERIMENTS WITH ALCHEMY

After *Principia*, Newton was ready to venture into new directions, thus, he diverted his attention to different fields of study. During this time, Newton served two times as the Member of Parliament and represented Cambridge University.

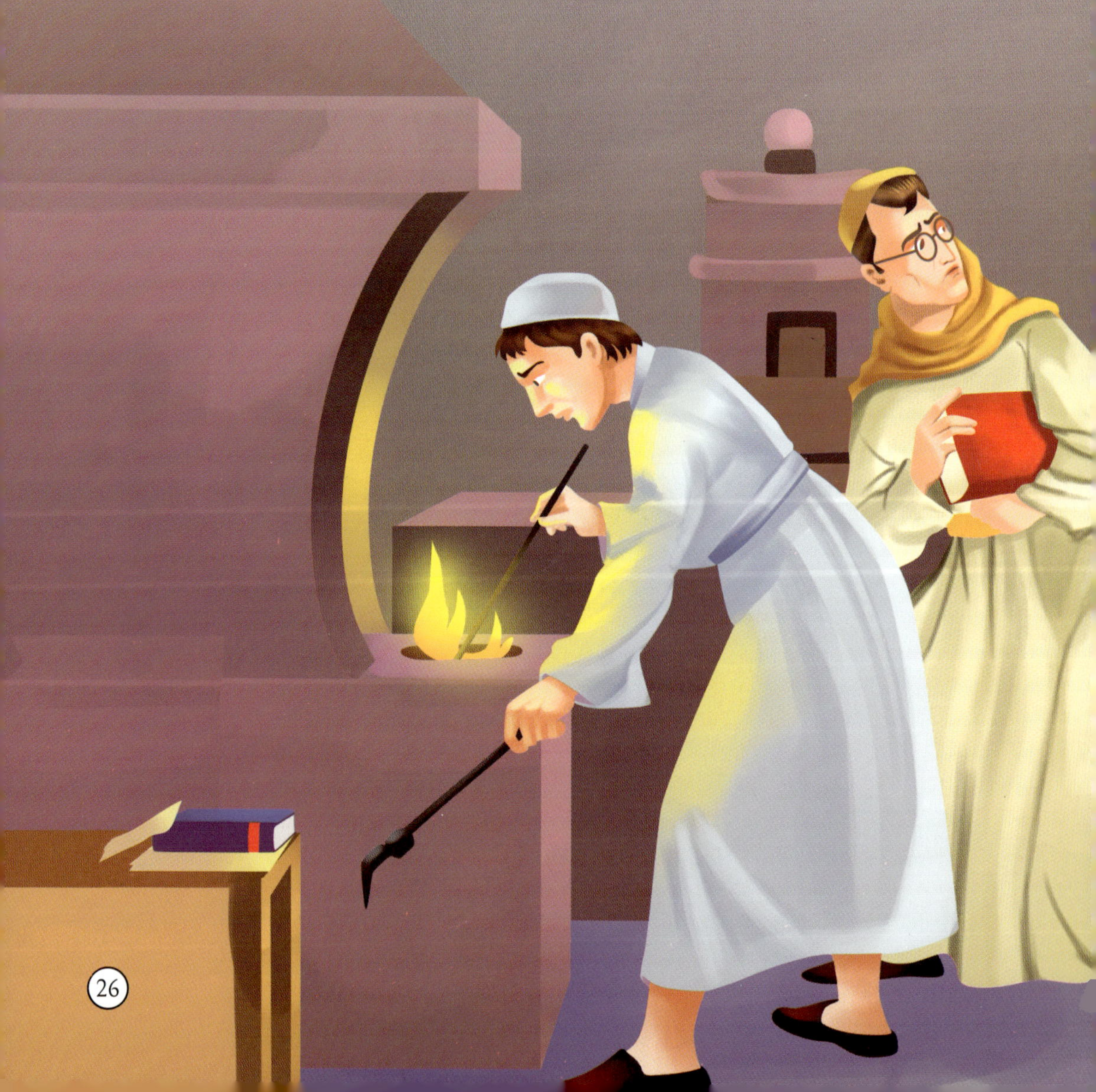

He also indulged himself in the study of alchemy and biblical chronology. But unfortunately, the majority of his work in these fields remains unpublished.

During this time, diverse fields were opening up for experiments, and scientists were indulging in all forms of studies. Intellectuals were grappled with not only the discoveries of modern science but were also venturing into untapped dimensions in order to discern a wide range of subjects.

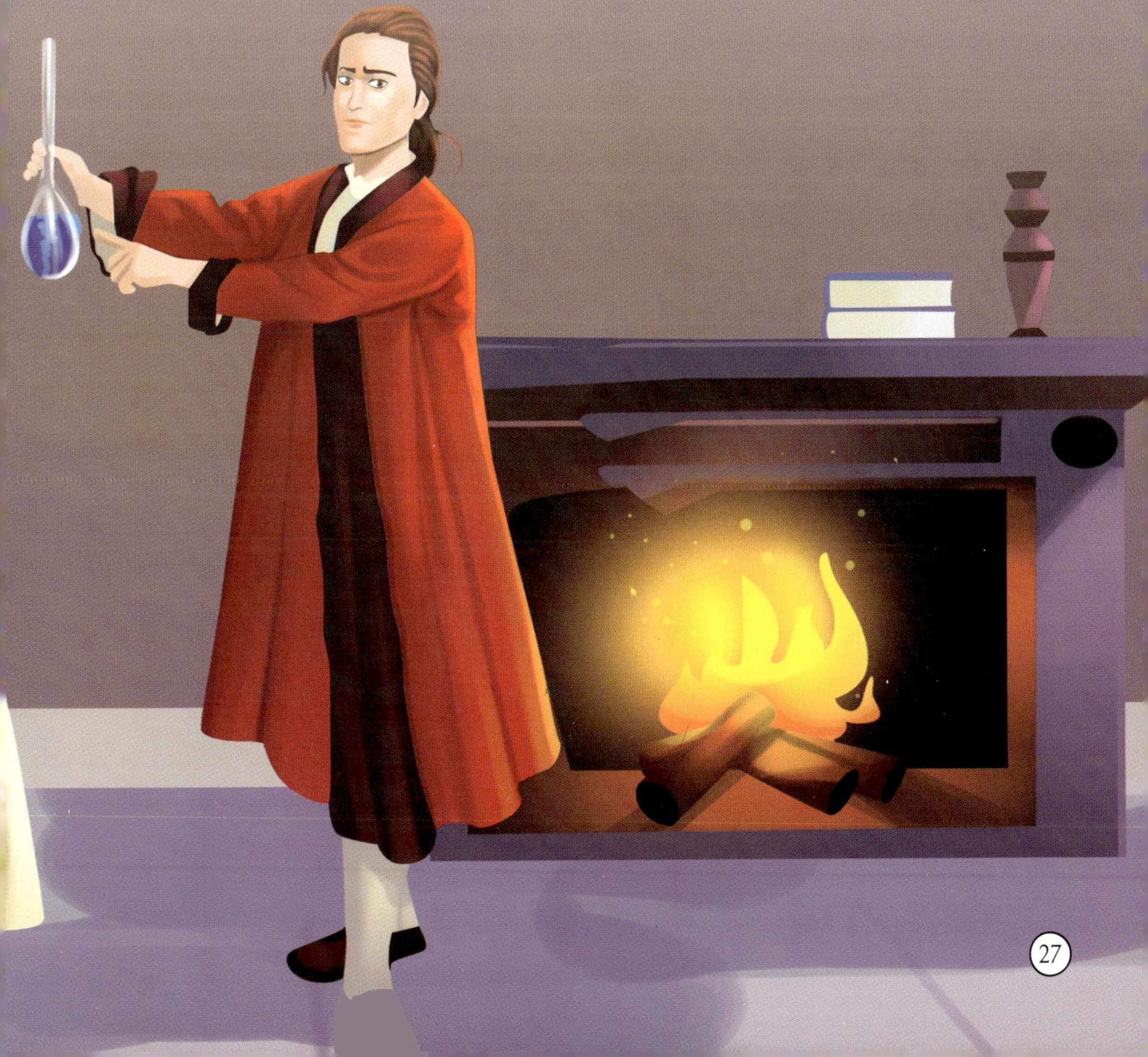

REACHING NEW HEIGHTS

In 1696, Newton became the warden of Britain's Royal Mint, and as a warden and later as the master, he took his job very seriously. He brought strong reformations and took steps to severely punish the counterfeiters and clippers.

In 1705, he was knighted by Queen Anne during her royal visit to Cambridge University. By now he had amassed a fortune for

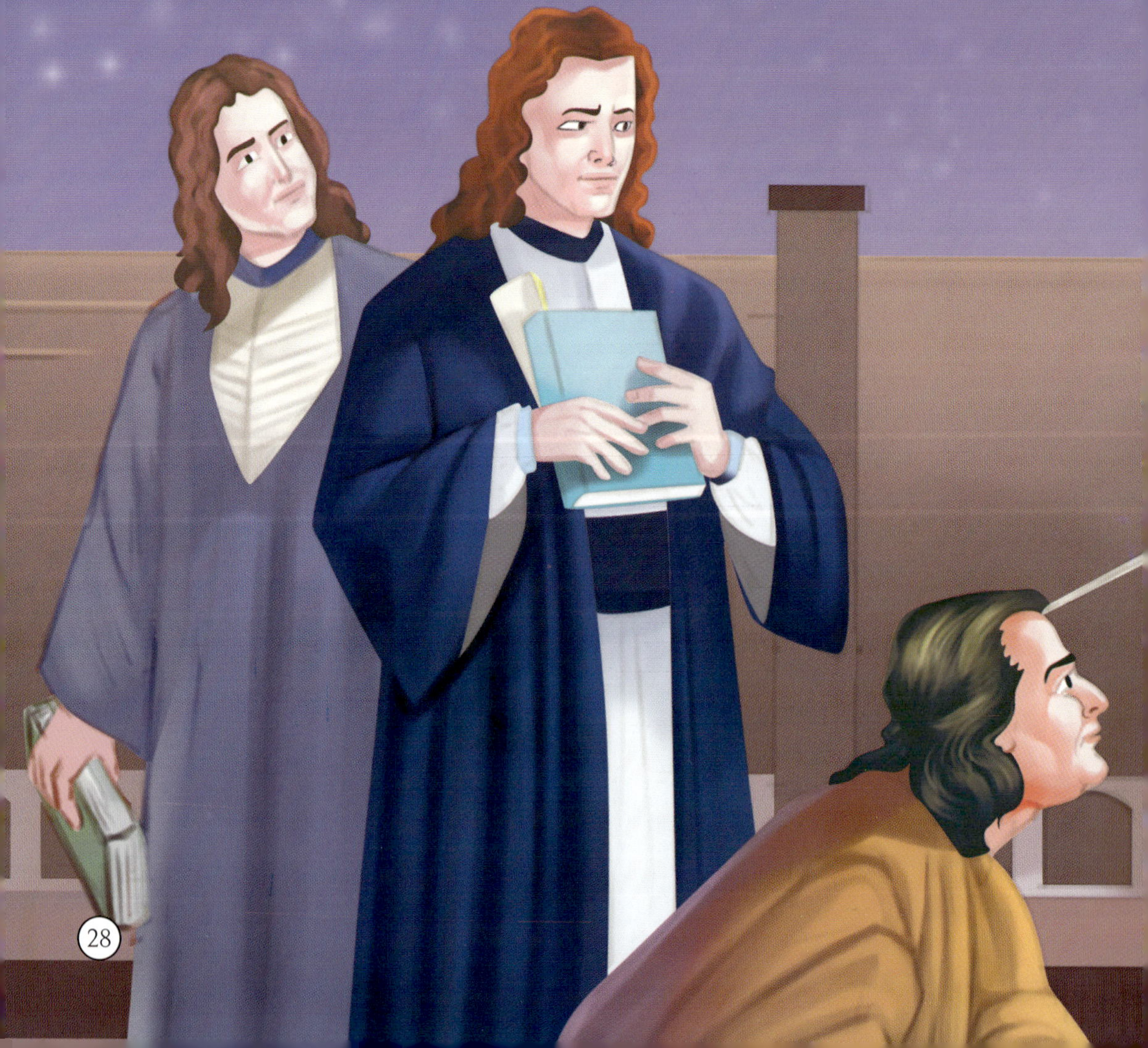

himself and acquired an unprecedented name and fame. In 1712, Newton went on to become the president of the Royal Society and was re-elected each year till his death.

Newton died in his sleep, at the age of 84, in London on 20 March 1727. He was given a grand funeral which was attended by intellectuals, scientists and nobles from all walks of life. His remains lay buried in Westminster Abbey.

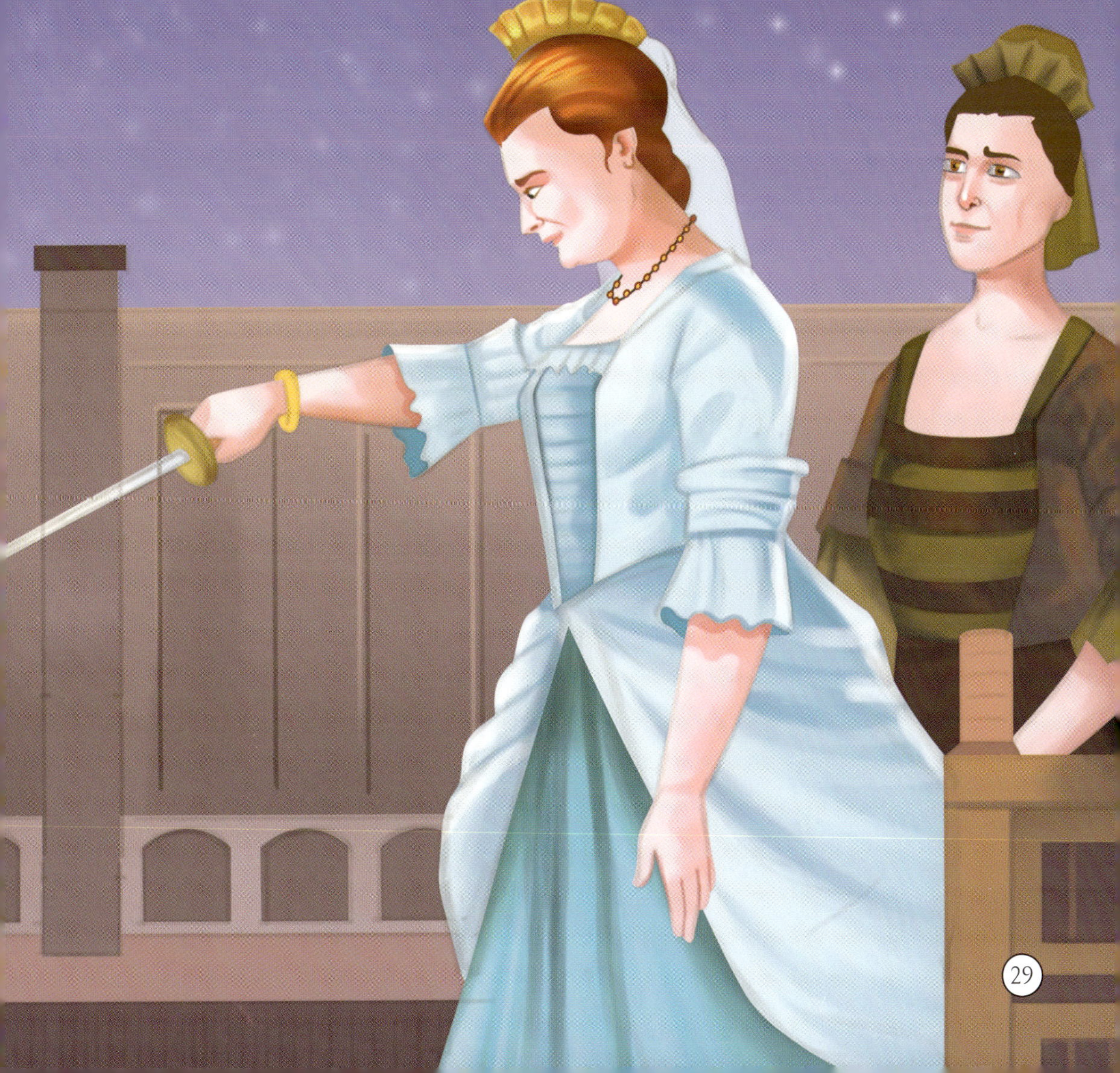

THE MARK OF A GENIUS

Newton is proclaimed as one of the greatest geniuses of all time. His fame grew leaps and bounds after his death. He famously said 'If I have seen further, it is because I stood on the shoulder of giants.'

He is nothing short of a colossal lighthouse shining its light into the mists of the future. He gave the world the precious gift of the law of universal gravitation, which is unparalleled. With his sheer brilliance, he unraveled the mysteries of the universe; while giving sense and reason to the basic phenomena, which we simply take for granted.

He describes his journey with these heartfelt words, 'I do not know what I may appear to the world; but to myself, I seem to have been only like a boy playing on the seashore and diverting myself now and then, in finding a smoother pebble or prettier shell than ordinary; while the great ocean of truth lay all undiscovered before me.'

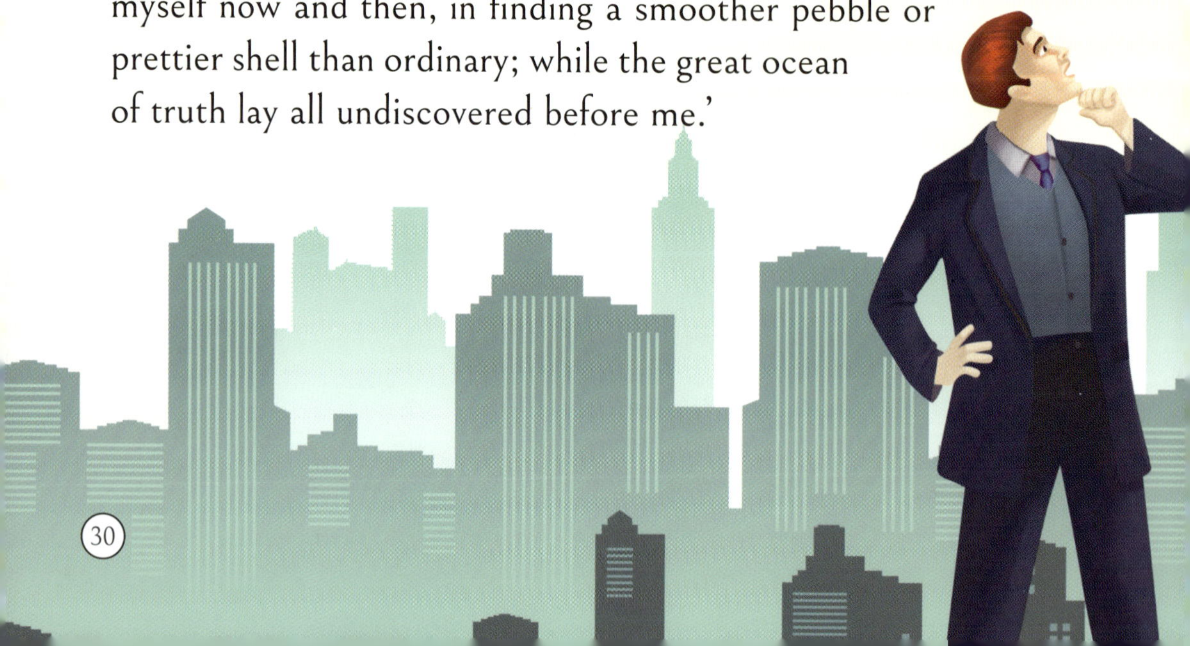

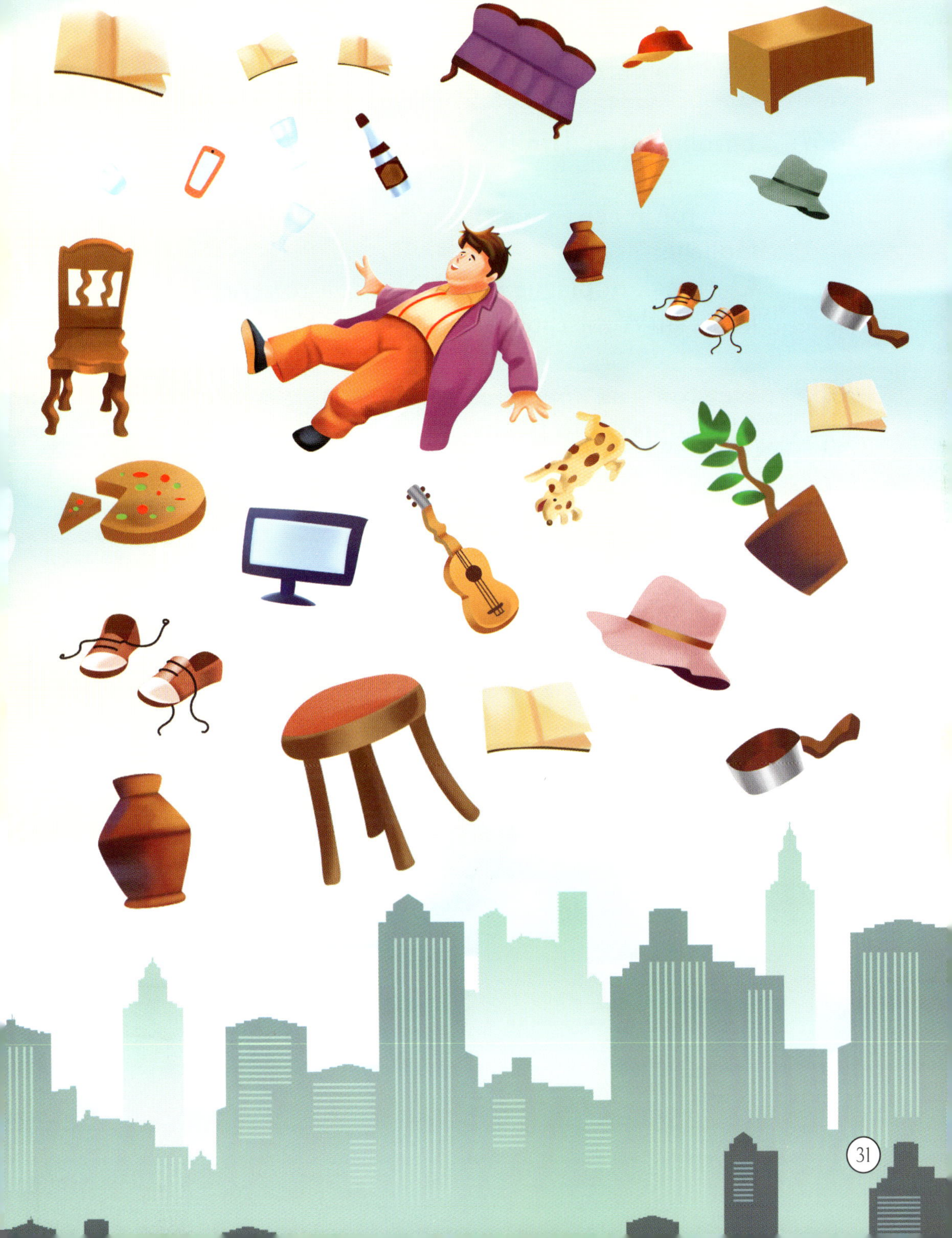

1643 : Birth of Isaac Newton in Woolsthorpe, England

1654 : Newton enrolls in the Grantham Grammar School

1661 : Enrollment in Trinity College, Cambridge

1665 : Newton receives his Bachelor of Arts from Trinity College;
Outbreak of plague drives Newton to retire to his home in Woolsthorpe

1669 : Newton gets appointed to Lucasian Chair of Mathematics at Trinity

1672 : Newton gets elected to the Royal Society

1687 : Publication of the complete *Principia*

1696 : Newton gets appointed as warden of the Mint

1704 : Publication of *Opticks*;
Beginning of feud with Leibniz

1705 : Newton knighted by Queen Anne

1727 : Death of Sir Isaac Newton in London